Words To Live By

Published by Pearhouse Press (pearhousepress.com),
Pittsburgh, Pennsylvania, in partnership with Impact Books.

IMPACT BOOKS is a registered trademark and is a division of Steve Gilliland, Inc.

Printed in the United States of America

ISBN: 978-0-9802355-7-9
Library of Congress Control Number: 2011908980

This book is available at a special quantity discount for bulk purchases, for sales promotions, premiums, fundraising and educational use. Special versions or book excerpts can also be created to fit specific needs.

For more information, please write:
Impact Books, 2801 Freeport Road, Natrona Heights, PA 15065
or call 1-866.445.5452

Words To Live By

A Book of Inspiration
& Quotable Wisdom

STEVE GILLILAND

PEARHOUSE
PRESS

INTRODUCTION

*M*any great things have been said by many great people. Many are wise, many are funny and some are both. For all who believe that the pen and the tongue is mightier than the sword, I can guarantee that you will savor this collection of my words of wisdom. In this book are assembled thought-provoking sentiments from my two best-selling books, ***Enjoy The Ride*™** and ***Making a Difference*™**. This collection of quotes and wit is designed to inspire and motivate, to encourage and lift up. ***Words To Live By*™** is from my heart to yours. I trust these words will impact you and those you share them with in a very positive way.

— *Steve Gilliland*

Put all you have into all you do.

Every parent, coach or teacher says the same thing, "All I ask is that you give me your best effort." If you put all you have into whatever you do, you won't eliminate failure. If you put everything you have into everything you do, you won't eliminate disappointment. So, why bother? When your personal philosophy is to do your best, regardless, you will always stand tall in your own estimation. Losing hurts, but it hurts even more when you realize that you haven't done your best.

You may not always make right decisions. However, you have the ability to make a decision and then make it right.

Don't squander time being angry
about the circumstances you're in.
Be curious about how you got there.

Regret preoccupies you in ways
that will demoralize you and
your ability to let go of the
past and improve your future.

The certainty of any circumstance
can disclose a fact that will not
permit you to wholly believe
it which ultimately directs you
to repeat the same mistakes.

Being willing to ask the tough question isn't the hard part. It is having the guts to answer the question honestly.

Common characteristics you admire
in other people are something
you see as a deficiency in yourself.

Making a difference requires you to merge your ego with the aspiration of your soul.

Focus your efforts on what you can change and accept what you cannot.

Find people whose personalities and achievements stimulate, fascinate and inspire you; then strive to duplicate their patterns of superiority.

When you don't believe in yourself,
you expect the worst, not only
of yourself, but of others.

Forgive everyone for everything.

When we choose to forgive as we change, others change. As we alter our attitude toward others, they begin to alter their behavior. The moment we choose to change the way we see things, others respond to our changed expectations. The hardest person to forgive is ourself. When we blame God, others or ourselves, we are avoiding the real issue which is the need to do something about the problem. We can get on with our lives and live in the now, or we can chain ourselves to grudges and upsets of the past.

Accepting instruction from people is a life-changing choice that will help you break away from your own negative thinking and allow you to grow.

A major detour in your journey
is allowing destructive
emotions to consume your
energy and make you negative.

Your destiny will not be tied to anyone
who is willing to walk out of your life.

It is better to live your own destiny imperfectly than to live an imitation of somebody else's life with perfection.

We can make choices that will provide
us with opportunities to enjoy the ride
and afford all that was meant for us.

Find your purpose. Define it and make it the core of what drives you.

We let others define and,
in some cases, limit our
potential to be successful.

A dream will provide you
with a reason to go, a path
to follow and a target to hit.

Success is attained in inches,
not miles.

All of our dreams can come true if
we have the courage to pursue them.

How you see yourself performing in certain situations is a result of how you believe. What you think, you are.

People who make a difference
don't look for achievements that
will bring them the most with
the least amount of effort.

Choose a job you love and you will
never have to work a day in your life.

The good times make you smile, and the tough times make you thankful.

Tough times allow you to reexamine
your life's work and your calling.

People who make a difference do not
fall prey to procrastination.

You have to break your dependence
on a standard of living that you are
comfortable with and sometimes take
a step backward to move forward.

The road to regret is besieged with
overlooked chances.

Opportunity is a mindset that ignites
the passion within you!

We are constantly granted
the opportunity and mandate
to grow, to learn, to change.

People who are committed to a
purpose usually view change as a
challenge rather than a threat and
aren't stressed by it in a negative way.

A good self-image allows us to concentrate on compliments paid to us and the successes we have achieved.

Our self-image determines our focus or what we allow ourselves to think about. Being egotistical and having a healthy self-love are complete opposites. People with huge egos need to be the center of attention, crave recognition and have little concern for those around them. When we genuinely appreciate our own worth, there is no need to tell the world how good we are. It is the person who hasn't convinced himself of his own worth who proceeds to inform the rest of humanity of his worth.

Don't put your umbrella up until
it rains. Worry restricts your ability
to think and act effectively.

We become what we think,
and our perception of any event
will determine our reaction to it.

In every experience you have,
find something good. Life is about
perspective. The glass is half empty
or half full depending on whether
you are drinking or pouring.

Doubt your doubts,
not your beliefs.

Allow the changes you go through
in life to make pressure an ally.

The key to growing will be your
ability to check your passion
every day and never lose it.

Why you do what you do provides
the motivation for doing it.

We have managed to take the
inconsequential and make it important
by making it more immediate.

Your ideas, thoughts, information,
activities and insights are the
means to seizing the opportunities
which may pass you by if you
don't expand who you are.

Success is deciding what you like
to do and then determining how
to be successful doing it.

Life is worthless unless you give it value.

Life in itself has no value. Just because we are here does not mean that our lives have any value. Ultimately, only we decide whether our stay on this planet is to be our privilege and our joy or whether it is to be a sentence of misery and despair. Life is not dull. Some people see beauty and magic everywhere they look while others remain unmoved. No matter how much beauty and magic you have enjoyed up until now, you can choose to have more fun today. It is a choice, every day.

However good or bad a situation is,
it will change.

No matter how you feel, get up,
dress up and show up.

Make peace with your past so
it won't spoil the present.

Generate and maintain a burning
desire for your purpose.

The most important opinion you will
ever have is the one in your head.

When we admit our mistakes
and make amends for them,
we reclaim our power and
actually like ourselves better.

At the end of our lives, who we are
and what that has contributed to
the process of making a difference in
people's lives will be more important
than anything we have produced or
done for money, fame or power.

When we think we know it all,
we miss the point.

When we are self-centered,
deep down we believe that if we
did not create it or make it happen,
it simply does not exist.

The process of forgiveness is one
of the most important processes we
can learn in life, with self-forgiveness
being perhaps the most difficult of all.

Your mind will give back exactly what you put in it.

Whatever we don't use, we lose. If you decide to spend three years in a wheelchair for no other reason except that you like sitting down, you won't be able to walk. Stop using your legs and they stop working. We have to keep using our mind to keep it in shape. There is no reason we should become less able as the years go by. If we keep using our mental capacity to the fullest, our mind will keep working for us.

You shouldn't judge your potential
or ultimate success or failure
by the first win or loss.

When we are pretending to be something or someone we are not, we cannot help but feel uneasy.

Sometimes the things we are
most passionate about escape us
not because of a lack of talent,
but rather because we lack the
resolve necessary to pursue them.

The small stuff makes a big difference!

The people who make the biggest difference in your life are not the ones with the most credentials, the most money or the most awards. They are simply the ones who care the most.

You have not lived a perfect day,
even though you have earned
your money, unless you have
done something for someone who
will never be able to repay you.

How empty our words are when they
are not sustained by our actions.

Wealth is enjoying what we already
have, not getting more of what
we think will make us happy.

Very few people acquire wealth
in such a manner as to
receive pleasure from it.

True wealth and stature come
from depth, not height.

Be questioned for who you are, rather than believed for who you are not.

My mom, being a Baptist, cringes when I tell the joke about the difference between a Baptist and a Methodist. A Methodist will say hello to you in the liquor store. A Baptist will hide behind the potato chip rack. Translation—be true to you.

In order to be an inspiration to someone else, you have to be inspired.

Imagine what might come up
if we shared our thankfulness at
dinner every day and turned a
holiday tradition into a way of life.

What you do for yourself dies with you.
What you do for others is immortal.

Your influence will either
be positive or negative.

A lone person you influence positively today has the potential to influence thousands of people tomorrow.

One man practicing sportsmanship
is far better than fifty preaching it.

People who have been down so long will try to recruit you to stay down with them. Since they are no longer interested in getting up, their goal in life is to pull someone else down to make themselves feel better.

A true friend prods you to personal
growth and stretches you
to your full potential.

Becoming the leader sometimes
creates emotional distance,
yet it is imperative for you
to be your authentic self.

It is your life experiences that open up
your heart to have compassion for the
most difficult challenges that people
face along the journey.

A point of view is worth 80 IQ points.

Margaret Shannon, my former secretary, taught me to always let others bring out the best in me. She believed that the more perspective you have on any subject or situation, the better decision you will make. Several perspectives allow you to see things from a variety of viewpoints. Remember—none of us is as smart as all of us.

It is impossible to unselfishly
give of ourselves without
being blessed in return.

While people are motivated by several factors, it's the emotional component that ultimately influences people.

Without vision,
you have no direction.
Without direction,
you have no purpose.

If you want to impact people and make a difference, your number one priority should be building trust.

Your actions and your image of
yourself are inextricably linked.

You create what happens to
you based on your decisions.
You create your future both by
your actions and your inactions.

Never let your surroundings or
circumstances control your attitude.

The amount we earn or the
success we achieve produces
emptiness unless it is in line with
a purpose beyond ourselves.

Life may not be the party we
hoped for, but while we're
here we should dance.

Your life's work can be found where
God's plan intersects with your passion.

We attract what we fear.

Because the things that we most love and most fear tend to occupy our thoughts much of the time, we tend to attract those very things. Yet most people stagger through life bemoaning what they don't have and talking about what they don't want. It is a hopeless situation. We must focus on what we want. When we fear losing something, we place ourselves in a position to lose it. This applies to husbands, girlfriends, wallets, tennis matches and football games, etc. We often find that once we decide to face the fear, it evaporates. No doubt you have had the experience of performing a task you thought would be difficult or particularly embarrassing. When you jumped in and did it, it wasn't half as bad as you anticipated.

Don't fear what you want the most.

Love what you do and, most
importantly, why you do it.

Abundance is the result of
appreciation, not accumulation.

We purchase things we don't need,
with money we don't have, to impress
people we don't even like.

You will never leave where you
are until you decide where
you would rather be.

The trip is more enjoyable if you
know where you're going.

There are no limits in life.

Make "now" the most
interesting time of all.

Live more for today, less for tomorrow
and never about yesterday.

If tomorrow never comes,
make sure you are satisfied
with the way today ended.

Life is not perfect.

Happiness is a decision based on making the most of what we've got. The degree of our unhappiness is the distance between the way things are and the way they "ought" to be. If we cease to demand that things be perfect, the business of being happy becomes easier.

Start from where you are now.

For every sixty seconds you're angry,
you lose one minute of happiness.

By always chasing after another "there"
you are never really appreciating
what you already have right here.

It's not the broken strings that stop you; it's your inability to see what you have left to play.

At the fork in the road, turn "right."

For every action or event,
there is an accompanying lesson
that must be learned.

Lesson learned. Wisdom earned.

Discipline is doing what you really
don't want to do so you can do
what you really do want to do.

The mastery of life is the mastery of self.

Human growth is a process of arriving at the fork in the road and, through experimentation, trial and error, ultimately finding wisdom.

Things crumble with the erosion of values.

From television to radio, the classroom to the boardroom, our values have decayed to a point where nothing is surprising anymore. Company mission statements have become nothing more than fancy decorations strategically hung in visible places for people to see. Values will always reveal what you care about and what you stand for.

Compassion opens limitless doors
to human connection.

No one can ruin your day
without your permission.

Adversity will help you decide
what you really believe.

Life picks on everyone…
don't take it personally.

Our attitude determines
our approach to life.

Most days you will not get what you
want; some days you will only get
what you need; but every day
you will get what you expect.

Nothing is as contagious
as an example.

You are everything you choose to be.

The greatest thing you will ever learn
is to use what you learn.

Comparison prohibits you
from seeing your uniqueness.

Leadership is taking people where they have never been.

If you're going to take someone where they have never been, it might be a good idea to go there first. Too many times we fall victim to the leadership theory of "the lost leading the lost." We expect people to follow us. Yet, when we are not sure of the direction, we frustrate ourselves and everyone else in the process. If you're not sure where you are heading, you will get where you are going—nowhere!

Never be content with someone
else's definition of you.

No one can make you feel inferior
without your consent.

We learn to no longer believe the
dreams we dreamed as children,
because we dare to be different.

What you decide to do next will
determine what you do next.

Revealing of feelings is
the beginning of healing.

To thoroughly enjoy the ride,
you must first learn that you can't
make the entire trip in a day.

Decide what's important
and never take it for granted.

Never let the urgent get in
the way of the important.

Love doesn't make the world go
around, but it sure makes the trip
a whole lot more exciting.

Life provides every opportunity
to get it right.

A "will be" is a "has been" in progress.

If you listen to every person in life who says, "You can't," then you will never leave where you are. Become a "has been" who embraces the attitude of "I will be" and "I believe I can" to emerge as a person who "has done it." Our job isn't to judge other people on where they have been, but rather to encourage them in what they can become. Everything in life is a process that, through trial and error, helps us progress to the next plateau.

Time is irreversible and irreplaceable.

The most precious things in life cannot
be built by hand or bought by man.

Instead of taking prayer out of
something, put it before everything.

You can't change people.
You can only influence them.

When you spend time doing
something someone else can do,
you won't have time to do
what only you can do.

Compassion gallops.
Judgment merely walks.

Confrontation is a positive way
to handle negative events.

Behavior not confronted
never changes.

Follow the talent you have been given.

Give, not in the spirit of obligation or debt, but merely in the spirit of service.

Clarity is the perspective you can't see.

The glass is either half empty or half full, depending on whether you are drinking or pouring. I learned early in life that there is no reality, only perspective. What a person sees, or perceives to see, is their reality. In leadership, the greatest gift to perspective is clarity. Searching and finding the truth allows you to gain a perspective that may otherwise elude you and distort your reality.

Courage is being scared and then
doing the thing you think you can't do.

Don't go through life.
Grow through life.

Instead of preaching a sermon,
become one.

If you don't believe in yourself,
very few others will.

If you fail to plan,
you're planning to fail.

Life is short.
Enjoy the ride!

Don't worry because a rival imitates you. As long as he follows in your tracks, he can't pass you.

If we do not learn humility,
we will learn humiliation.

Steve Gilliland (The Speaker)

Steve Gilliland is one of the most in-demand and top-rated speakers in North America. He has been working with meeting planners and speakers bureaus since 1999 to entertain, educate and inspire audiences all over the world. Recognized by his peers as a master storyteller and brilliant comedian, his appeal transcends barriers of age, culture and occupation. Steve's interactive and entertaining style helps audiences connect and relate as he shows them how to open doors to success in their careers, their relationships and their lives. He speaks to more than 250,000 people a year and has shared the platform with numerous dignitaries. Over two million people have heard him speak, with his audiences crossing over 29 different industries. Steve has the distinction of speaking in all 50 states and in 15 countries. As one newspaper stated, "Steve is what happens when the humor of Ron White collides with the inspiration of Zig Ziglar."

Steve Gilliland (The Author)

In addition to his brilliant speaking career, Steve is an accomplished author. His book **_Enjoy The Ride_™** has been on the publisher's best seller list for five consecutive years. He was named Author of the Year in 2010. His thought-provoking writing style makes his articles a favorite with nationally prominent magazines. He influences the lives of millions through his keynote speeches, books, CDs and DVDs. An extensive array of these products has been utilized by small businesses, Fortune 500 companies, U.S. and Canadian government agencies, churches, school districts and nonprofit organizations. Speaking the language of active business leaders, his books and CDs identify practical lessons that grow people and their businesses.

Steve Gilliland (The Businessman)

Steve built a multimillion-dollar company from the ground up on the same philosophy he expounds to his audiences. If you continually learn more about your company, your industry, your customer and yourself, you will always be a leader. You will be purpose-driven rather than process-driven, and you will make a difference. His motto is straightforward: "If you take care of people, the business will follow." Implementing this principle, he has helped people grow their businesses and expand their lives by teaching them to rethink their work, their relationships and themselves. He was recognized by Who's Who for Speakers and Business Professionals, and his company was acknowledged by the "Pittsburgh Business Times" as one of the fastest growing privately held companies in the region.

Steve Gilliland (The Person)

Steve was born in Pittsburgh, Pennsylvania, lives in North Carolina and travels the world. He graduated from Butler High School (PA) and received his bachelor's degree from Grove City College (PA). He is a proud grandpa, devoted father of four boys and a loving husband to his wife, Diane. Steve learned great compassion for people and a commitment to a hard work and balanced life ethic at the knee of his highly principled Christian mother and stepfather. Whether Steve is speaking at an event, writing about current issues that impact people or leading his own employees, he is not just a person who challenges people to change, he motivates them to do so.

Other Resources by Steve Gilliland

	Book	Audio Book	CD	DVD
Enjoy The Ride	✓	✓	✓	✓
Making a Difference	✓	✓	✓	✓
Performance Essentials in the Workplace	✓			
A Treasury of Motivation (6 CDs)			✓	
Hits of Humor	✓		✓	